A LESSON
FROM THE
CYCLOPS

and other poems

A Lesson from
the Cyclops
and other poems

RAPHAEL RUDNIK

Vintage Books
A Division of Random House
New York

First Vintage Books Edition, September 1969

Some of these poems appeared originally in *The Centennial Review, For Now, New Directions 16,* and *Quarterly Review of Literature.* The poems "The Lady in the Barber Shop" and "Penny Trumpet," appeared originally in *The New Yorker.*

Library of Congress Catalog Card Number: 72–85595

Manufactured in the United States of America

To my parents,
Amalia and Charles Rudnik

CONTENTS

I / A LETTER FOR EMILY

Morning Song	3
Images Lost in Chicago	5
The Painting of "Flora"	6
A Letter for Emily	8
Charity Dinner	11
Instructions for Social Investigators	12
A Jealous Extra in Macbeth	13
Race-Track Fable	15
Love, Like a Landscape	16
The Death of Sardanapalus	17
The Airport	18
A Good to Be Endured	19

II / A LESSON FROM THE CYCLOPS

A Memorable Fancy   23

Baal   24

The Lady in the Barbershop   30

The Target   33

Eclogues   36

A Lesson from the Cyclops   44

Daphne   46

An Old Man in Wild Woods   47

Fires   48

Manuscript Found Under a Mattress in a Hotel Room   49

III / ACTS

Two Flowers   61

Waking Up   62

A Sentimental Journey with Albert Ryder   64

Walking Out   65

Penny Trumpet   66

Aftermath   68

The Sound   69

On a Traffic Island with a Stranger   70

Execution   71

Acts   72

Mothy in the Mind   73

Moog's Bar on Snugglepuppy Road   80

I

✳

A LETTER FOR
EMILY

Morning Song

You said we would wake when it was still dark. Tips
Of a tree light gold above brown running down
Like thickening sand. A cage of spines
On the ground is moving its curved lines
And blossom and blossom and blossom—one
Whiteness until wind shifts, cutting strange strips,
Puffing hoods falling into flowsy blows—
Flowers are dying a little outside.

I dreamt you were a flower next to *He:*
Good-natured six-foot spider, green cap,
Guarding a black gate by the sea. Before
He reached you you grew through in (and therefore
Because of) the time it took to work up
Into sweetly sensual mockery
In language the only thing he knows:
"Flowers are babies that love to die outside!"

The work that lovers do never has to wait
For a boat-full of flowers coming on sea
As brass fanfare blares the willing retreat
Of spiders and milky emulsions meet
To make a moon against night. Love, we
(Take it from me though the word love is late)
Should not even delay till darkness shows
Through the glass vault of sky dying outside.

I want the breath that is in air you breathe.
At first you seemed too small, almost a boy,
Then *there*—a blossom floating up and
Up a tree (looking infantile, bland)
Turned into the color-kissing joy
Of light! Soon there was nothing to our breath
But what it touched and owned, slackened like those
Flowers asleep in their death-cage outside.

Your back seems to haul the first light. Now where
The round red squad of powers turn you
And I are one thing that can only say
We will always thank God for day, the day!
I look back at time and I see you.
Your goodness has slept in my body where
It woke this morning song, hurtling homeward close
To what once gone will make us die outside.

Images Lost in Chicago

Made of morbid particular fineness,
Like serial bits of Time,
Dark clouds drift, massively, yet alone.

And yet more marvellous, above them, is the raw
Thin riotous blue, whose furor is a dream.

The Painting of "Flora"

So good is he who paints me, my dull
Pride almost made me think he sighed
For my growing age. As if he could tell,
Or even remember that my freshness has died.
It is the cold, grey pearls which line
My skin, that sad bargain of leaves
Pinned to the black hat-brim, and dulled, fine
Fruits which trouble him. I do not make him grieve.
Yet I know these things will not be displayed
On me, in paint, to make me what I am not.
Nor have I that look for which finery is made:
Graceful, solemn and deliberate.

Today is called the Devil's Day, and now
Across the square, the children dress in bright, old cloth
For the church's miracle play, and allow
Their friends to dress them in the rough
Colors bought from us. Now they touch, caress,
And paint the play's faces. There is no flesh
Beneath that brightness for them. As they kiss,
They kiss their own creation: Time, with a thresh;
The Devil with a gay box of husked souls,
Dry as my hat leaves; or Innocence,
A girl with golden hair. She trips and falls
On a small dog there . . . or was it Arrogance?

The ashen, purple light begins to cover them.
Now, they'll light a flame and begin the play.
Maybe her name was Eve. Adam
Or God will condemn her for losing her way
On the small beast's guile. I will play Eve
This while, ignorant of what she must believe:
A handful of fruit; musty green things
On a hat that shades no sun; bloodless rings
Of pearl; and a new covering of cloth
Usurping the fallen flesh. His love
Of this strange world has grown much
More than for the body he learned to touch.

Yet let him paint in this, my look, that cloth
Will be to me as passionate and as rough
As his fingers and eye were—both taken
To make the fruit and leaves whole again.

A Letter for Emily

I mount chill steps, endless, small and cold
As words with which the end of love was told.
The bootlegger slat-lock hangs from the door.
Green hall-light flings in upon ruinous plaster.
Outside, in strict blackness, a frail luminary clock
Of moon rides still and blind above a black
Tree, whose boughs are great spears that quiver
As if to shoot out in the pulling wind. A shiver
Rends them beautiful, where upwards, they grow thin.
Orange neon breaks upon all like rotting sun.
Here Emily, your golden hair was all my sight,
Spun through your flesh and the morning light;
My sight teaching care and love to my mind
Toward our animals of love which labored blind.

A lipstick scrawl reads: ONE HOUR AGO
ONE OF THE CREATURES OF THIS WORLD WENT BE-
     LOW—
THAT IS WHAT CHRIST MEANS! Our neighbor's mind
Finally delivered itself! She stumbled in, half-blind,
The day after you left, rounded her arm, and stole
The cat. A pure theft of love. I wonder her soul
Could write this, and do that. Now I hear her snore
Or mutter Finnish wisdom to *Misshuganah.*
Do a cat's moods change when it changes masters?
With us it had no sense of sin. You would smooth its hairs,
And it would willfully half-sleep, wanting to keep
Both the pleasure of your touch, and of sleep.
Poor uneasy half-soul, lost between two pleasures!

Yet he would come to us when we were most sure
Silent and happy. No matter, he is dead to me,
Magician of the nine times you rejected me.
The tenth time he stole all our love and went free.

A picture still clings to the wall: I see you and me,
Without our friend, in Cranach's *Eden*. Not white flesh, nor age,
Nor light of God changes Eve's eyes, but jealous rage
At ragged leaves eating an infinite sky.
Only the serpent seems himself and is free.
His element is spent. Eyes cut back in pain to cry—
Adam hunches—wants to throw those branches to the sky.
Spirit and taste of man fruit and beast make Eve show
She loves herself by loving what she does not know.

I hear the vendor's voice: self-breeding as dirt itself,
Gluttonous and full as fruit rotting on our shelf,
Sounding up the hollow, baffling steps to the sky
Where the luminous green church dome rises cruelly.
Caught between cry and cross, the soul of this place,
In monument-shaped tenements, cannot efface
Their disparate greed and anger. Without emotion,
They rise high as feet can climb for food and sleep alone.
I dreamt once we were bounded so: your dancer spirit in a shoe;
And I in a pen, which was sedentary and slow.

Remember that store downstairs with one great gold fish
Twenty times the size of twenty silver fish?
He lolled there like a cool, dusty flower,
Darted, gripped a tail and held. The tiny flower
Sank dead at once. Or did it pretend to die?
Ah, what pretense could make it rise, with that eye

And mouth moving above? He always held with care
The ones which struggled in short, lovely shivers,
And, as they struggled, bit further and further.
The whole tank seems to me now a chill metaphor
For hell, with this slightly favoring morality:
The ones struggling to die seemed more free.
Yet our blessed fierce old woman goes to church to see great
Plaster saints with devouring eyes. She must appreciate
A good look at them. They are holy because they
Return her look hugely, but in just her own way.

I feel love in writing this to you, but not
Love wholly. As in our life I fear that it
Will be ruined by my words and the world I put in it.
A moonlit Platonic frenzy mocks me from the lot:
Brown, incandescent crusts of detritus and oil,
The obliterating dream of moonlight on tin-foil,
Prove beauty grows from the worst, if the worst accumulate:
Though all foul stench is there, and cracked leaves whisper in it.

The moon is clouded and near as my pain.
Now sky releases a calm, perpetual rain.
I'll shut the door on that, ending with images that started me:
A bare, killing dark cannot create the identity
Of what it loves; gold and white without dross
Will not let me mourn this place as part of loss.

Written to you in my twenty-second year,
leaving my first true world like a beggar,
who, losing all his love, cannot love all
familiar looks of chaos which become law.

Charity Dinner

Giving her great good, Charity clasps
To beggar Rhetoric, who flies with a moan
Of mortals eating their flesh and bone.

So immense is the buzz of that golden fly
Filling the room—the ingenuous sleep
Of the secretary's hum breaks like glacial winks
From the thousand-glassed, swaying chandelier.
Steaks, cigars, brandy, varicosities
Of flesh disappear in a horn of smoke . . .
Diaphanous red hair, milky skin in green silk
Sings the very termites from out the banquet-table
While sleepy eyelids mambo with the talons of their
        wives . . .
Generations go back into blankness of
White record-paper's transparent membrane:

"Wallmaker, Horn, Goldstone, Isaacson"—Once
Marching to a sum of whiteness just beyond their sight,
The sons of Isaac brought a stone of gold
That broke upon the fragile wall of God.

Instructions for Social Investigators

The rusting green eyes of sealed-up domes
Have nothing to do with people.
Sleeping huddles—homeless, hurt and late—bums
Have nothing to do with people.
As you climb up the stairs, echoing corridors
Have nothing to do with people,
And dogs' angry, involuntary roars
Have nothing to do with people.
You open the door. Its gold number falls.
Have nothing to do with people.
Bright bulb's crazy energy, white slant walls
Have nothing to do with people.
Mirrors inside reflecting their own crash
Have nothing to do with people,
But seem to dissemble the same tragic wish:
Have nothing to do with people.
This is no trap. There is no enemy.
Have nothing to do with people,
And they are gone. Nor does the solitary
Have nothing to do with people.
See your brown bag. Its yellow affidavits
Have nothing to do with people
But have bruised lovely families and wits.
Have nothing to do with people
And the room and the voice and the record
Have nothing to do with people.
Till you are all the emptiness you hoard,
Have nothing to do with people.

A Jealous Extra in Macbeth

Where are our lovely things? *The play's the thing,*
With which to catch the conscience of a thing!
I strip off my First Lord's elastic leg-bands,
Rush to the love-scene's side-spot, wash my hands
In yellow light, sleighting an effect
Of wavering passion. Macbeth comes, erect
And immersed, taking his preparation
From an empty cup, grumbles he is done.
I've rattled the thunder-sheet, banged the drum
To start this scene and see Macbeth come
Turning the haunting splendor of my days
Of love into lustful gestures he plays!
Now the roaring whirr of the curtain
Bursts the scene open like my sense of sin.
See scum-colored sequins stud her gold dress!
See the light race her coils, black tress on tress!
Purity is in the act, she says. Those
Who act are clean friends. This dog-ape closes
On her night and day, rehearses and does.
On-stage they kiss. His eyes, hardly mates,
Wince womanly, harden to furious fates
Baring the part she needs. I prattle and pule
Loud off-stage lines. The double-bodied thrall
Of their last words signals laughing wings
To blanket them. The rushing curtain sings.
Before they part the boy-man-king shrugs
Her to his hips and one last kiss drugs
Promise of bed where actor-spirit feeds
Off love my murderous jealousy breeds.

The fake, forgotten cup lies on the stage.
My hands lock in it, drunk with their own rage.
I must change now to a sad, anonymous man
At the banquet-scene, lamenting dead Duncan.
(His trick-thrill of voice, dismembered beard out
Again.) I always cry when the king shouts:
"Our monuments shall be the maws of kites"
For her mouth rouges his mouth through the night.
O fierce, unremembering love—
Outside, on black bay-water, you move—
Breaking core on core of cold light, making more
Lonely singing for bell-buoys by the shore!

Race-Track Fable

The mad runt brought his whip through air,
Circling wildly, chiding the air:
"Ballast of hell . . . stuffless statue . . .
Endlessly imprisoned woe!"

Auguring, oscillating black cores
Fell. A stone man on a stone horse
Stood the course. Imperious, blind
Silks and hair mingled in the wind.

Love, Like a Landscape

Love, like a landscape, is painfully
Renewed by an eye which dwells alone
On the city. Yet it has grown,
As in the night this waterfall goes to sea
While no human eye perceives its might.
So your face is a secret discipline
For my absent, dreaming eye during night,
Which day and its features can only refine.

Love is neither green leaf, nor green landscape,
But poignant attendance to one green thing—
Never ending in summer. The scattering
Bushes break dull brown and seem to escape
Into shadow, but the flat horizon
Is broken by bushes that curve and lead on.

The Death of Sardanapalus

FROM THE PAINTING BY DELACROIX

My whip made her hair a maundering mess.
And that horse she was strapped into, useless—
Only white eyes and his sweet breath to her.
What are the standards guarding my bed for?
Now cut white silk of that skin not worth life.
Shall endless endeavors to lose a wife
To my eunuchs amputate my will? Kill
Her gentlemen, or one of you I will.
Thrust deep as life is sharp on innocence
So I may study limits of her sense.
Not in my bed where she has been bad! Turn,
Turn her head as you hang it from her hair.
Cleanly severed, she wants to see me burn
For a body indifferent as air.

The Airport

The tiny flying-machine spreads its wings
Across the brown flood in my coffee-cup
As if waiting some Master to rig it up
Again, and make it fly—or other things.

Whatever the plans it could try, it drowns.
I saw too slow to save. Infinite sky
Stilled, rushing traffic filled my quick eye.
Or was it to see how a poor fly atones?

Staying his mad design's relentless pace,
A larger fly cannot decide to land
Anywhere now but on my face, my hand;
Buzzing bare sound as if in disgrace—

Then tuning so fine, fortunate and free.
The owner brushing this godless table
Bends his bald head, ignores a raw fable
From me: *"Did he dine here—St. Exupéry?"*

A Good To Be Endured

The wind was blowing coldly through the hotel-lobby.
"You mean that English lady—poetry is her hobby?
She's gone, *today*. Sailed. Too bad," the clerk kissed out. *"Muse,"*
I screamed, frightening him, *"thank you for this gift I cannot
    refuse."*

"Such brazening despair. Now you shield your face
With both hands, while your mouth works ghostly dental-floss,"
He leered, "but your last face will be total collapse—
Total except for this:" (he gave watery slaps

With his tongue like some dithering, brain-destroyed dog.)
"Clerk" I cried out, making him stop, "have you the Log
Of people she saw, and the dates?" "Oh is *that* all you want,"
The pimp giggled, "names of the other participants?

I'm not at liberty to give that or you to get it
And until you live here Raphael Rudnik, forget it—
Or at least forgive," he ended with a wince, then blink, then wink.
How he knew all I was and about her! I could not think

And was sleepily nodding. Like a nurse
Not terribly concerned with the patient (me) but the force
Of a sickness, I almost forgot my pain—
Since sickness kills, not pain. "It is very plain

You must sign here." I was surprised. The clerk's eyes
Blazed opaquely like wine in a frosted glass. "Size?"
"Of what," I murmured. He showed a paper. "Size of your line.
It is clear we have to know for how long you sign."

"Sign? But why has she left me here all alone. I have no will.
Why does she appear like a ghost, then tear my heart and go?" A
     thrill
Went through that solitary, half-dead man when
I drew a length and wrote my name at: *love is signified therein.*

II

A LESSON FROM
THE CYCLOPS

A Memorable Fancy

ATOMIC BAR. Dark, though open. Dark-glassed,
Steel-wool tufts of hair *diabolique,* a
Violinist played. A black cat stared at
Labyrinths of a pinball machine,

Yawned. The same silver string of spit
That whore made asking if I was a man.
"Yes" I said, "and you are a flower
Opening brilliantly at the bottom

Of the sea, shutting in its hollow stalk."
"La nuit, hein?" She pursued the musical man
Then, kissing the coins in his cap (every one)
Dropping the faces upon each other.

Baal

TO AUDREY NICHOLSON

As his pants open, Baal has time to laugh
At the orbic flex swallowing his stuff:
"Like God, I see my seeing, in your eyes,
Then all our other senses synchronize
My broomstick in your toilet. What a prize!"

      *   *   *

Baal while watching a vulture overhead
Hears what the vulture in his skull has said:
*"Play dead. That body like a bunch of bloody knives
Will land on you in the last of its dives!"*

"Into each life a little brain must fall!"
Says Baal, wiping feathers from his smile.

      *   *   *

Baal made his way into the bleeding roots
Of sex, and saw a man hanging there
Upside down. His heavy hanging hair
Moved like little wings in the still air.
Baal harvested him with hand and foot—
Shot after shot into the heart till death.
"If the caught root of heaven will not dance"—
"If the caught root—" Baal sang, regaining breath—
"Will not dance, hanging by foot is Circumstance."

      *   *   *

Another sample of Baalian woo:
"A belly is as bad as a breast that low."

                    *   *   *
On the parapet he pinches to push
Into her struggling mound. With a rush
Flesh was manipulating its traditional
Two guises. The flower in her hair seemed
Crooked, tired—as if it had grown through. Baal
Saw the river go by and he dreamed
A fantasy as good as the moon
Above hurtling milky emulsions:
Hollow coils of an abandoned bed-spring
Glittering on dark, moving depths: sound
Of a bird whose nest is drowned singing
Until its life and his are one sound.

On the shut bank at dawn he saw with hate
A piece of raw meat stuffed in a sewer-grate.
                    *   *   *
"Egocentrifugal" all men vex
Baal into ruling out a whole sex.
                    *   *   *
Baal wants to have a machine with a hook.
Baal wants to use it to publish a book
About what goes into publishing books
And how such ventures are related to hooks.
Everything functional except the scream
That wakes the reader to another dream.
                    *   *   *
Baal bent over a bridge on a river
At night. The air woke with a shiver.
Thirty-three bottles in his brown bag.
He dropped them one by one. Shuddering drag

Of foam, sound like cymbals, silence.
"One for each year, a ritual pretense"
Baal told police who had been drawn like
Shadows through the silent streets to strike
A bomber from the bridge. They booked Baal:
"Disturbing the peace. Manner exceptional."
"I wanted to see blue coats, gold buttons
On black water breaking white foam
Like my green bottles, but those cold muttons
Were pale as vampires—" he sang, going home.

*　　*　　*

Between exalted mountains Baal stands.
Lack of passion makes his praying hands
Dream of each other, and the high altar
Of the snows reminds him of how far
Breasts go. The ground grumbles hungrily to
His knees. He kneels until he can go.
(Everything in a church excites him past
Believing in anything but his lust.)

*　　*　　*

He knows he cannot follow the sad lovers.
However freshly she may stand Baal sees
Her silence is as in a fruit that hovers
When its own ripe fullness longs to be free.
And yet they walk hand in hand quietly
Each the other's garden. Sometimes they look
Reminded of their joy, then jealously
Baal would purge all light the sun has struck.
But they live naked in that gold and pure.
Her dark hair measures it, while his hand
Touches brightness only he can reassure.
Unused the green leaves under which they stand.

Baal is what they pass. They pass with winged dread
That seems to pierce till soaring overhead.

$*$ $*$ $*$

Baal dreamt of a fountain with an arrow
Moving up and down like a decoy bird.
And he was happy to see the thing harrow
Catacombing furrows of water. *Baal-bird*
Baal-bird sang the sessile hush of water,
As if he were going on the water.

$*$ $*$ $*$

"I like cold ham, but you can't cook pussy!"
Ruined near the white and bright, the metal sea,
Naked as the empty sky, and throbbing,
The girl whose body Baal was robbing

Placed her pale form under a wave, lay down,
Centering the world into a small death.
What had Baal to do with being that could drown
When one wet kiss beat into its breath?

Then her dead flesh became a living wall
Too large to kiss or hold, strike or defile,
And Baal could not wander from that wall.
As at birth, he was a spinal ball.

Till his zipper smiled, catapulting out
The limbless, faceless man. Her flesh did not recoil.
White stuff gestured like a clown—ruined, devout.
A black gleam left his ass, murmuring *Baal!*

The white wall grew a ghostly ghastly hole,
Orbicular mouth flexing a silent laugh.
Undone and undoing as her soul
The body spoke its own loud epitaph.

In that leaping shine of flesh Baal could see
Her soul—a big white opening rose. The sea,
Like the leaping-sign of flesh was horror,
A bright edge torn spirit took as mirror.

"Rigged now in heaven with hair guyed to the pivot
Prick on which our vacuum turns—the one pin
Every bitch here burns to become hot
On, and burst like a stray balloon in sun!"

Strike, soothe, and teach her what he was, he must,
But her skin no longer shrilled in the dust
And water—only brain-like cabbage lolled.
Comedian Death, a black dressed dandy

Picked up the faceless thing and ate and strolled
By the white and bright, the metal sea.

*   *   *

"I like the smell" Baal said to a crouching blur;
Believing it watermelon-rind, sea, not her.

*   *   *

"Now we are in the black forest, and now
Things get interesting because broken snow
Will fall and the fox with bright brown berries
For eyes will watch night grow clustered stars,
And he will rise to taste the light—
All because I killed a man tonight!"

See the shards of stone all lift
From ground as from the whole earth's curve,
And stone angels looks stunned drift
Undefined as the self's nerve—

And further in a blue green red
Maze of flowers a white head
Lifts to the sun as if all dread
Could be lost where light is led.

And further a little stone child
Glowers at you from oblivion
And Baal sits weeping, limbs still wild,
And his dagger red in the flesh and bone.

* * *

"Wait, wait little smile" was Baal's last song.
Swaying in his calmest eagerness he hung.

The Lady in the Barbershop

Finally, among the bottles shining,
The manicurist makes a fine thing
Of her hair—black satin horse's tail
Insatiably growing from her frail
Oriental skull—she braids a coronet
Out of the dark wave. The muse of wet
Wavering lines tightly wound to a net

Of form makes measures men must forget
Because so soon changed, not out of regret,
Or rearing back, or forgetfulness,
But for simple delight black tress on tress
Can be changed. This garden of herself
Spread on her bed at night is her pelf
And her dream, and is a dream itself:

Sargasso where a lingering sea-sylph
Floats downward with seaweed into a gulf
Of great naked rock that is safe and alone
Shining there like some lesser moon.
She makes her appeal to the starlit hours
That draw the tides of this dream: "O Powers
Of night, when I wake and the flowers

Of my hair, seen here, where baldness glowers,
Neither sun nor moon, but the thing that sours
Men and is unknown—let it be seen
On their heads' deracinated heaven,
And let it be my hair that is given,
And my head riven. The world is bald,
Not just they, yet they need to be told."

But the flaming swords of Times Square
Break with the morning on her black hair,
And her mirror is a wilderness of fires
Unsought, like inconsequent desires
Of men. Who has followed her home or has
Gloried in watching her aqueous
Mild glittering among bottles and mirrors

Is on her mind then. How sad the scars
On the head that thinks, "It was, it was!"
The no-faced moon near each cuticle
She will cut in the day is strange, is cruel
As unknown pale privacy
Of stones in a cemetery
And forgotten as they. But "To be, to be"

Each dying filigree seems to sigh,
And as it falls she thinks, "It must hate me."
What to make of this hell where men are wise
That the world falling past their eyes
Will not come again, yet is owned by her?
Ah, all her bright imaginings blur
When she looks in the mirror and sees her hair.

Who can think of justice when it is clear
Celebration is the only thing one can bear?
She sweeps herself up into the line
Of darkness that is her discipline.

The Target

How is it that when he had wrought his sense
Upon the ragged fragments of the time,
A head of steel with myth-hungry eyes
Appeared as our target—taking prize
Every industrious soul that could climb
To shoot a center with lucid violence?

II

Bright, triumphant look and gun in the room
Of a mind that was gone. There the madman
Shot again and again space shots spanned
To the car. The man waving his hand
Fisted it in fear, fell on the woman,
Ripening fast blood into martyrdom.

III

Then a brave body swaddled in blood
Interpreted all substance enmity,
Even hating herself for roseate spots
Flowing through her heart. How he had hit
Finally from a height in the city
Only the executioner understood.

IV

Office-windows, like open, shining graves
Showed death glittering in fragile evidences.
A man disturbed asking him. Not to lie,
He took out a small gun and made him die.
*"There are no shields behind the senses
Of people blank democracy depraves!"*

V

Trees involved in their own statuary.
Flags, sentinels, dogs. A raving siren
Made his brain a seething corridor
With bodies, bullet-battered on the floor.
And then in the dark, upon a moving screen
Soldiers fought; surging near a bright sea.

VI

Statues skidded off their pedestals,
And came to him with guns in silhouette.
Jammed there, they kicked him in the head. He
Cried: *"There is no freedom in the country!
In such a place there is nothing to get.
In such disgrace no vows are made by souls."*

VII

Assassin saw a smoky medallion
Of moon, prayed it would shine into his cell.
He bared his breast to it. The fragile stuff
Came and covered him, easy and enough.
He knew that he was something that could kill,
Yet loved life enough for a million suns.

VIII

Glimmering stone hid life like a bone.
Moonlight was a metaphor for food
On fingers. Sweet pink stones he sucked
Until he licked the line where they had locked
Around the gun-stock. There he heard blood
Roar as if it wanted to be alone.

IX

Then shadows came to beat and question.
Cold beer-cans glowed golden crescents
That pierced him, causing the cold-crazed cry:
"Answering unanswered answerings, I!"
Moon wrecked clouds. Raffish insects marched. Silence.
He slept soon, darkening his last sky. Sun:

X

Silent, bodiless fluttering working in
Shut eyes. One opens as rage, one distress.
Black centers move circles of color
And see that emptiness can blur
Into night with endless pain to confess.
And only a steel bullet smiling on.

Eclogues

"And have you come to yourself clear, since she has gone?"

"Let me enjoy these spirits, these forlorn creatures
That are flying about my head."

                "They are the leaves rain
Has washed down after the long drought."

                  "No, they are fresh—
Even though they have not been born, or have been undone.
They have lives and colors like a tomb airlessly passed
By time, that is pried open and blazes for a moment
Till wounding air tightens the color to ash and skins
Turn into brown paper."

          "Are these spirits of your love?"

"Flitting phantasmagoria: little flower-ends; a fish
Whose fin is his proud identity; broken round of a crown;
Long diverse greynesses, workers from another planet—"

"This is strange love."

         "All love is strange until lived in."

"What do they tend to?"

         "If our bodies were together, real

Spirit between us would be an inexpressible child
Setting our limbs growing wild till one day it gained flesh—
These are probably the natural life of that child, smithereened
By lost place and time."

　　　　　　　　"Why do you pick that tiny yellow?"

"Because goldenness was once all I could see. Another love."

"The design has not left it yet."

　　　　　　　　"Now all the life
It can wish for is in this tiny, perfect flower."

"The petals still shine."

　　　　　　　　"Within an hour, it will be dead."

I I

"Is the flower gone?"

　　　　　　　　"My breath blew it out of my hand
And then wind took it."

　　　　　　　　"A decent burial. How are
Your friends, the unknowns?"

　　　　　　　　"Who?"

"Flower-butts, conceited fish,
Mars Local 1, cracked pointless crown."

"Salt kills small creatures
I suppose."

"In other words love cried them to death.
The things are dead, long live the queen! What is she like?"

"She is white and ruddy."

"A redhead then.
But why are you so slack and dull—do you want the gold one back?
You always want to hear me crank up my questions?
Why are you suffering?"

"I was quiet and controlled
Myself more than I even thought I should, but blood
Wants to touch blood, and rage requires sunk mouths tongued out
        of space,
Dumb glowing."

"What has that to do with being where?"

"Bleak turns lettered with club-footed serifs: EXIT
(Bleak turns littered with club-footed seraphs. Exit!)
Led me to her door. She opened slowly, widening
The wedge of darkness. Little mirroring vanities
On the table gave wet points of light like eyes in the sea.
She had a deep and coral red that glowed within her soft white bed.
Her body was broken by mirroring scars
And shiny black wrinkles like lead. When we were one,

38

A hard white cup dented where the handle had broken off,
And an accumulating saucer, stuck together—what had I done?"

"Not much. But your miniature man, the faceless, limbless one,
Probably murdered the blind and winged one
For the time being."

           "Shall I write to my love,
And tell her what I have done?"

                "You have done nothing
But smiled in your sleep."

                "When I got out at dawn it seemed
Everyone in the world had gone—"

                  "They had—to sleep.
Like you, they needed to."

              "Would she forgive?"

                  "Come along
These endless trees and forget what you've been through."

III

"I heard that slut sigh, through my faint sleeping:
'Ah, this lighthouse-keeping!'"

              "Lighthouse-keeping?"

"Lighthouse-keeping. Now, listen to the dream
That leapt out of me then."

          "But why sigh, 'Light . . . ?' "

"Strange, I know—but she did. So. I saw a great beast
Which had been ripped, held whole, saved—changed
Into a colored clay cliff washed brilliant by sea.
Wind broke off a red spar that fell, bringing red
Into an immaculate pool. I said:
'You have done everything, can be everything but flesh,'
Gratefully painting my flesh with wet clay.
Wind shook—"

         "The lighthouse!"

                  "Silence. It was next, at night
Turning red and white. Someone climbed the glass like a fly
In a liquid of light. Under cycling air, a small sign read:
'State Road Ends Here'—and on its sea-ward side:
'State Road Begins Here.' Beyond, a long white island, a knife-
       blade
Between dark sea and horizon pierced
By fog-bound blades of light. 'Young man,' a strange voice sang.
I saw an old Indian on a pile of wood—
Wielding a black cane topped by a brass claw
That gripped a glass globe reflecting light
With the same forlorn mildness he had in his eye. 'Young man,
Why is it linen will get whiter laid in the sun,
But a man will get darker? Because *I* am the man,'
He crazily answered himself, growing closer—
'Why is that white island called No-Man's-Land?'

He intoned through a garlic-shaped nose. 'I suppose,' I started—
'Silence!' he boomed, shaking white hair stiff as a whisk-broom.
'Because it has gigantic Government shapes, Government
Builds, grows tired of, bombs, shaking blocks
Of sacred cliff down.' He pulled at his eyes till
One grew red and one white. *'See my ball-bearing ring,'* he
    screamed
(Almost too violently to continue to be dreamed).
Ring rested on sceptre. 'I punched the clock too late.
Factory docked me cost of these things. *Fate,'*
He laughed, 'is an unstolen glass globe.' The globe seemed
To grow swollen with light mixed in it from overhead,
Pieced together little dark faces gay with feathers, shattered—
'That is Injustice growing tired of Race,' he roared, then
Sea-whispered to me: 'Look in my eyes.' He had grown close
    enough
To show the white one untidy with veins, the red
Shut by a white lid. 'Red will riot and rot
Color like the great cliff which is the last thing seen
In life. The blood-stream bursts into all shapes
It was not before becoming black clay in the ground.
White is the partition of hate that closes each race—
The all-colored white of hate.' His lips prepared a kiss. I woke
A little. The dream broke around its first phrase again: 'Ah,
This lighthouse-keeping!' Then it began
A new, last voice: *'There is no bright vessel*
Or mysterious minister here, transforming
Ordinary cheapness and laughter. And why should there be?
Winter comes, laying its linen sheet the madman
Said sun could not change. Soon the road loses the strange

Centering white line—has only white, red flash from overhead.'
White, red flesh from overhead. The voice turned into her sucking
     moan
Like surf on stones. A live ash fell on my hand
From her cigarette glowing in the dark, real room.
My hand crawled away. Her touch was only dust and pain."

*"Light-house*keeping!"

                    "Damn it, again? We've clinched that point!"

"Light-housekeeping, scramble-brain. *Not* gigantic domesticity."

"OH, I see! I knew what she said meant nothing to me!"

"Nothing in thought or view. Only a dream of a wrong world."

        I V

"The first motion of love is so gentle."

                    "Tell it—"

"The descent to the falls seemed in the wrong place.
I remembered it near a path further in.
Aged, indifferent stuff—now smooth, now rough—swam
A pond I last saw with a girl in blank cold:
Snow under boots then—*duh duh*—strange green ice.
Dry leaves skated strangely. 'Old languages

Without soil?' 'My country has snow-topped mountains,
Jungles, sea.' 'It has everything then?' 'No.'
Water poured into water in the last
Of the falls where everything is mirrored.
She showed a tree whose roots had fused strange grey
Smoothness the curve of the ground it entered.
Blood in my arm tapped softly. I wanted
To touch her. 'I'm pawing the ground' she said.
A languageless, colorless, imageless
Being loved everything she did and said.
Tree: a white wedding-gown. The rising road
Seemed gently lifted by its grassy spine.
Her voice rose, hit and fixed the hollow roar
Of the waterfall: 'My life goes like this road!'
Over her body's immeasurable poise
Darkened ends of long red hair trembled.
The straight smooth tree shone white except where sun
Gave red or gold freckles, brass-colored outlines.
A lorn, thin face of moon, self-mirroring.
Thick trees blackened vast, smooth gold sky whitening
As if it would melt from within. Twigs snapped
Under me. Each breaking sound and substance
Seemed a word and touch given without her.
Increased dark and cold gave a sense of time.
We spoke of someone 'fallen but not fell'
Through bad things . . . so 'bitter—warm and far.'
Friendlier than her face, her plump poised hands.
Earth stopped spinning in toy-like complacency.
Hope hummed in me through the tree-shaped nerves and
Places without metaphor. I loved her.' "

A Lesson from the Cyclops

(CYCLOPS SPEAKS)

Pulley-cry from the fallen boy
"Got a red-eye, never had a red-eye."

With haughty, dreaming looks
And arm still rounded from the throw that struck
I spoke "Red-eye? Your eye is going back!"
Then danced through the glistening playground
Of my wishes without sound.

Grass blades sprung back.
The tawny field was dyed
Red, where the boy got up terrible-eyed—

What was and what
Will be his sight divided his face—
A hardening plug,
Like peppermint-striped toothpaste
Then like the penis of a cat;
And an eye.

He pulled out a Beatle-wig,
Put it on,
Singing *"When I'm gone"*
He went on
Past my stone

Smiling in a patch of green, rouged
By blood whose grip once gouged
From endlessly opening sky,
Fire-balling *eye*.

His small hands
Tried to block understand-
Ing
Winged stone like slow
Clouds covering
Yellow eternity.
No-no, no-no.

Swallowed him up so . . . yes, and learned
That time present as my scar—
Insane, particular—
Will be burned
(When I'm gone)
By a stone
Red-eye.

Daphne

What could he do to leave as bare leaves grew

Kissing clasped red buds grown above blue-
Veined whiteness already terrible, true—

What did he do to leave, as air leaves dew?

An Old Man in Wild Woods

FOR THE DEATH OF ROBERT FROST

Attending to a cabin in the woods
Where wedded life can have some real peace
Away from everything but leaves and trees,
All at once it seems the pines have hoods.
Then naked arrows whistle speed. Ah why
Do those savages labor to make me die?
Long brown wands of guns in our trunk
Among dried hair, flowers, memorabilia junk,
Found and fixed to fire. But will shots kiss
Off charmed rocks ravaging our vistaed bliss?
Too many outside to die. Trialing
Ancient weapons. I hide the wedding-rings,
Glorious in gathering darkness here.
Give my gun my unremitting care.
Work leaf-sounds from my lips. Wish light spun
To a strange world to the side of the sun.
In all these have so good a companion
As any red youth there. Most surely the one
Whom I will kill when they come for me.
So sure no other will implore, as he
Sets his breast glistening in my door.
Mild little jackal-laugh, of help so sure.
A man must make indignant defense
Of manhood against cruel indifference.
I will have his body shudder a star
Of blood that whispers and drums age and war.

Fires

Prometheus was unchained, confessed—
While red Easter dawned in the west.

Now there is a man who wants to fire
Spirit torn on visible edges of things.

Manuscript Found Under a Mattress in a Hotel Room

FOR THER AS WONT TO WALKEN WAS AN ELF,
THER WALKETH NOW THE LIMITOUR HIMSELF
* * *
THER IS NOON OTHER INCUBUS BUT HE—
The Wife of Bath's Tale

"What kind of room is it? It's a *room*."
His grey eyes seemed to look through me till
I saw them watching the effect of that,
And then became consciously unclear
While the mouth-edges worked as if torn
By fear. He mumbled: "Fellow, I want
You should meet a friend of mine, wife here—"
He opened the door a wedge and balked.
I could see the mayor on TV smiling
Over her pneumatic thigh flexing
A popped knee with dim blue butterfly
Tattooed on it. The sound was off and she
Sucked her teeth sharply in a kind of lavish,
Sensual ingratitude. "She's a real lady—
No cooking if you take it—give me that key
Monkey!" Her dress flashed in and out of view
Like an enormous feather writhing on fire.
Her face shone perspiration like a rash
Below massed hair curlers with white thistledown
Caught in each coil. The key shone flat in his hand.
"Top floor—first in the small back square right.
Come back quick, and tell us if you can take her!"

The wild music of her voice climbed with me
Up the stairs (each dark step seemed a clear
Consecutive abyss going higher):
"Is there no one here to shoot the man down
Like a dog? I sent for someone to kill
The rats, and his Inspector came with a bagged
Ferret—so what do you think happened?
The rats killed the ferret! I got a dead *ferret*."
Clouds, stars and colored buildings were painted
On the walls. The mayor should have sent an
Ardent allowance of air for the smell—
Depth within depth—as if a full ice-box
Powerless for a year had been opened.
The doors I passed were silent and still
As ones wreckers block off condemned buildings with.
I was thinking of nothing, literally
Nothing as I ended yet another
Walk in the forest of homelessness.
(It takes a heap of living to make a gnome!)
But the contact of the key and lock
Gave a small strange sense of being caught.

In the room: darkness, a desk, bed, window, chair.
The first and last ordinariness I saw there.
Now to set down in order the other things
That were there. "Your husband on toast"—a voice
Gave a kind of cheer. "Three cups of water"
Was the strangely logical-sounding answer.
But—"When they put me in a box and throw dust

On me"—next, didn't fit in, not at all!
Uneasy undertones, high false notes fought
Against my ear-drum—the voices beat
There like frantic, indignant insects!

Ear-dream. As if in answer, a square
Of cancelled light went on across the street.
The room leaned up like light-riddled air
On a highway at night. I thought of bright
Windows driven by at night—displayed like
Empty blazons of democracy, yielding
Nothing but loneliness, despair—people
Of air instead of pain, pity or love.
Then a strange stick with a head on it
Waved the head No from a window. *Me!*
It was my way of saying those people
Had no opinion and were simply there
And that was what was sad. Right. The light
Across the street went out. Another voice
Confirmed my no-opinion opinion
To the very genius of its gesture
By booming "God bless you!" Two more followed
Unplacated: "Baby baby, garbage
Garbage garbage—up and down stairs"—and
"You think when you die they're going to put
Pockets in your pants? No, they won't!" Silence

Learned its speech again. I don't know, but—
Don't take this too straight—the president
Was the next thing that happened. He appeared
I'm sure from a TV across the street.
His face stabbed through the darkness, mouth smiling

(I had not put the light on yet because
All above was minutes of pure distraction)
But lips grown big through the surfaces
Of glass between me and the TV
So he looked like some savage minstrel-king—
Longing to be free! It made sense to see
Him that way—as if I needed politic
Appraisal of a too-conditional state
And he shrewdly showed he knew my position
By becoming a symbol of it—
The loneliness of poetry. Then the eyes
Inflamed as though his glasses were burning
Openings into them and they bled
(Seemed to bleed) eye-beams in a pool on
The bed in the room. I pulled the light-cord fast
And saw first it had on its end a
Traffic-light. Tarnish dulled the trinket.
Now I was there and so was the room.

I don't know which number "thing" I'm up to
(Forget that black wing turning invisible
To my eye just then—TV winking out)
But the thing which came next was a *thing*.

It was a sort of spiral of light. Long
Loops led into more loops up where it had
No business being since the light was on.
My hair lifted, chill. "What are you—" I began.
Both ends of the thing fused down a little—
Cajoling, masterful. The room went dead,

Like landscape suddenly lost under cloud.
I thought that a blade of fire could cut it . . .
As if my life depended on it, I
Wanted a knife of fire to cut it! Somewhere
Above it some hissing seemed to dare it
And one end died down toward the floor pointing
At a mop that looked like a brain on
A purple spine. Words, *Mr. Swine* flashed through
My mind, then *ruffling white flesh of a pig*
There *put against a knife like wings going*
Across the sun, hovering, causing darkness.

The light-spiral seemed to take aim at me,
As if angered by an impulse to blame it
For more than I could know. Then it straightened
Like a white snake in a slot, pretending
To be a cornice-line. The room had none.
I knew it meant to show that there was more
Than a pig at stake, as more than a cornice.
I wondered if I could, should do anything,
And if I screamed would the thing go away
Or do what it wanted before they came?
Moving as if it had nothing to do with me
My hand pulled that traffic-scarab thing.

The light-line had not gained but lost some brightness
In dark, and was somehow slackening
Beyond slackness, like a rope preparing
Itself for sleep. I had no thoughts now
But the strangely new one of running out.
Mr. Swine, with reddening snout flew through
My mind and cold rocking below my hair

Like ice in a hot mouth, sighing: *Not fair,*
The rope bites, without sleep. My feet on the floor
Were standing asleep and my legs were
Backless shadows bending on the bed,
Which felt harder than a chair. Jumping down,
Jerking around me, the coiling light bound me
(As if I were an armature-core
Being forced to shine) and then a dark
Threshing ease spread up through and past my knees
Which groaned as if kneeling on the floor.
Another impersonal presence was now
In the room. This presence seemed to kiss
Air and free thoughts: *It didn't break me!*
Something with nothing to do with despair
Is freeing me into sleep that is good.

A sound I can never remember now,
Before the first moment of sleep. I dreamt
I slept in the room and dreamed of my body
Asleep on the bed which was more like
A little stage or an altar. In childhood,
Sometimes I went to sleep with a rope around me—
Wanting to dream of climbing mountains.
(Secretly, successfully in bright air!)
Now, in the dream I was tied that way.
Something knew that it could kill, and came
Invisibly around my throat. If I woke
I knew I would find it really there and
It would kill me in my dream if I slept!
I moaned in fear, frightening myself more
That the sound would wake me to what was making

Deadly, unremitting air. A new dream
Came: *into an empty cage, cleansed by time*
A pear-fruit grew: God had whitened all his suns
Into perfect edges of bone. Like spires
Of an unfinished cathedral, they cut the air—
Dessicate, immaculate—their own death's truth!
(Will what breathes and dies on those sharp knives of bone
Be known when heart and mind are bare as they?)
The fruit descended drawn by light from
The (bird-skeleton) *bones which were so sharp*
They seemed to impale sky like a blue beast.
As the light rose it turned into the sound
Of love upon the void of time: "O

I ache to wake up with somebody
Who has slept like the sun in my body,
And understands what I understand
As her hands move love like wands teaching wind
That loop and line are time and infinity—
My sharded throat the world's sweet earth and air."

"How long have you been horizontal?" The man
And his wife were above me. He winked
And slid half his face toward his nose slyly,
As if to show that anything goes,
Whatever I had done there was OK
With him, but not with her. I saw that I
Was awake, alive, as the blur of her
Ugliness cleared! The round head on her—
With tight white curls lying close—the eye-brows
Pencilled-in in three tiers—top two blurring

Into strange frowning mouth as she spoke:
"The pig-sty has charmed him and he runs in the muck!
I'm surprised we didn't find him here bare."
She grabbed the traffic-thing and seemed about
To pull. I imagined she would knock me
On the bed when darkness rolled through the room
And smother me with her body and breath!

But instead she blasted a sucking sound.
Now (*now*) I know it was heard before sleeping,
When it sounded like all of existence
Being taken by soul to sustain wayfaring
Far out on the brilliant desert of dreams!
Here her sound sounded like mouths mouthing
A restless hostage of soul for more food.

She plucked her hand from the string as if it burned
And spat. The trinket caught it, swinging free.
It clung round, yellow and white and bare
As boiled egg that had been shrunk by ice, then fell.
"Doesn't it go with the big eyes on her?" he
(Triumphant quiverings in her three frowns!)
Said grabbing a small glass bubble of water
From the desk. Two tiny boats raced
On the bottom. His trembling touch stirred up
Fake foam snowing all but air on top.
A plastic flower was down from its glass
On the desk. Filaments of light surrounded
Petals like cloud edges in purple dusk.

I needed a word from them, before leaving.

"You have a very nice place here, but you see
There are three of us, all bakers, and we
Would need a stove to practice on." She sucked
And spat again. I laughed and asked: "Do you
Get much light here?" He gave the word to me.
Distrustful stare, then: *"What do you want light for?"*

* * *

Trembling like a dog before unsure love,
I have barked it all out for a master
Who can make dark, heavy song light and light.

———————

The manuscript contained no more pages,
But enfolded this postcard, curiously
Unpostmarked: May 19, Dear Richard W—
It's a pleasure to have your manuscript,
As it was to meet you at BCU.
I'm grateful to you and Mr. Arthur for
Steering me toward the station, which I
Reached in ample time. Your MS is
On its way today to the first reader
Of our poetry board. With good wishes,
Richard W.

III

ACTS

Two Flowers

The soft white badge is on a stem which bears
Up with such stiff thickness that the single
Inflexible presence makes it seem air
And light managed to change and mingle
Into sweet stuff thrown atop a green world
That believed flowers are . . . merely flowers.
Next to it climbs a ladder of thorns, furled
Leaves shuddering momentary gestures,
Giving no support to a head pinwheeled,
Pinioned and perfumed by small sharp spurs
Of white that fit so tight they seem steeled,
And yet graced by a brightness like eyes
That know one petal gone the flower dies.

Waking Up

Every morning as I wake up
Over the brown flood of my coffee-cup
I look at Albert Ryder's *Pegasus,*
Or the Poet on Pegasus,
Entering the Realm of the Muses.

Impurities, uses
In the look between
Rider and gesturing queen—
His filleted face
Tries not to be seen
Searching her (unseen) face.

The horse he made race
Has an inaccessible spark
Of innocence in a dark
Eye, centering rocks
And sky.
      A big book
With broken pages seems to hold the hand
Of a Muse seated on sand.

In sworling tapestries
Of lace
Like moonlit rock,
Another,
The Mother-
Muse (below a black rock)
Mocks
Life she never had,

But is sad
That salutation
And love
Above
Cannot be forgotten

Because the bent wrist
And hand of the poet
Devote
And sing—
While the great, unfurling white silk-twist
Wings bring
Air
There.

A Sentimental Journey with Albert Ryder

Ryder leans on the rail. Bars
Disperse his sight, and stars.
He is leaving land behind,
As if growing blind.
The body of sea
Is big enough to see.

The moonlit cove moves the slow
Boat whose rail looks like a halo.

Walking Out

I walked out under a pale, solitary sun.
Wings were hands without a body. Smoke was the shadow
Of smoke. Words were wild things. A cat hopped out of
A garbage-can with a long, thin piece of yellow fish—
Mouth like a blinking eye, eye like a yawning mouth.

Naked knees were maps.
                              Twins with glasses, the children
Of The Cyclops.
                    This world may be the best one.

I saw her walking out, walking out today on Water
Street, watching wind blow burnt shreds of streamers
On a fire-escape, feeling her legs following her eyes
Into dead-end wall with many green shutters bending
Light like a strangely scattered deck of dead moths.

Then I followed her to where leaves like leaf-shadows looked over
A far flower-shaped crowd around a white machine
Playing tom-tom and trumpet music, singing:
"Want to be there, tell everybody!" Dark heads
Tipped bodies like swaying petals. A boy climbed
Up the music-truck, crouched a moment in staunch animal pride,
Then rose and bobbed and twisted like a happy valve—
"Enjoying the view or fixing to jump?" she asked me—

I stood embarrassed by her beauty, my world
Becoming private again—a newly painted altar.

Penny Trumpet

I had a dog like a love.
And once I had a cruel
Dream: she was a milk-pool
Around a penny trumpet.

I bought button-candy, bright
As bulbs on a high marquee.
My mind was like a movie
Of myself eating until—

Deep in the box—a penny
Trumpet like a lost light!
I stayed outside that night
In woods which were stained black,

And when the first light hauled
Itself up on its back, I heard
Proclaiming clock and bird
And played my penny trumpet.

And then I never stopped.
I played in every mood.
Till once, grass sang in my blood
While touching foot to top

With a girl who had no ear
For song and was not good
(Or so I understood).
The penny trumpet stayed

In my pants like a sunk boat
Trying to surface
Aright. Her face's
Remote, encircling lines

Broke in bars of light.
And her hard, feverish blooms—
Lips, breasts—led me to rooms
Where trumpets play all night.

Aftermath

The singing uproar cannot quarrel
Away that silhouette.
Although crumpled, wet and
Dwarfed on darkening sand—

Banderillas quivering—
Then a pinwheeling
Of ribbons revealing
Violent tremoring—

The bull on his knees
Shows prayer, not ritual:
A tree-root looking at trees
Growing past a canyon of skull.

Bring the sword on red cloud to cut
Behind his head, a small blow
Through the ear like dear Van Gogh,
And applause like flying smut!

The Sound

She did not seem to hear the sound or see
The missed train moving like a conveyor-
Belt of bricks on gleaming rails into trees.
Her hair was like rude fine grains of wood, her
Smile like suspended rails sparkling past where
Sounds echoed like the one I set free,
Shaking the green, embowelled machinery
Instead of the girl who said good-bye there.

On a Traffic-Island with a Stranger

She was dressed up to be
Pretty as flowers, stiff leaves
Uncurling underneath
Surf of petals.
                                        Somehow
Somewhere, we had been there
Before. But when we got close,

Her skin was like cigar-paper,
Body barrel-shaped on
Barrel-stave legs. She wiped
At her rouge as if afraid
Someone had kissed it there.
                                        We looked

At a strange falling
Yellow newspaper.
                                        Then she
Separated off into the distance . . .
Cars shot swift lights—
Painless attacks
On some boundary.

Execution

"Shall it be brought upon a banquet-plate?"
"Piked like a punctured drum. It grows late."

"The yellow bird that sings *weep-whips, weep-whips!*"
"Moths strike lit windows now like wood-chips."

"The killing muscles of my back are wings!"
"Do you wait for God to come see you do things?"

"I'll cut the tongue out before you are dead."
"Grieve me fiercely. Cut slow as if through wood."

Acts

Outside, unseen boys banging hollow, conscript cans, wildly
    singing.
"Things happen, and that is strange" I said. Her voice
Moved my lines against mad, slumbering noise
Emptying below: "Loving, the angel cannot see the world,
Nor can the world see it and be amazed." Then diamond-eyes

Invisibly darkened. *"Strange for an angel, but not our bare
Killing dark that cannot create the identity
Of what it loves, yet welcomes each chance to assert its pain!"*

My hand surrounded her warm hand, bare—
And looked like love, or what is done when there.

Mothy in the Mind

So he my friend, and she my would-be bride
Are dead, or gone—and Mothy crucified.
That dirty drug with which we quarreled
Insisted they leave me. Therefore Goddess, sing.

Past the last crude fence we saw dazzling
Images: in the glassy sun-spiked grass
Black cows grazing, then five red horses naked
(Standing and running, nuzzling grass and tree
And a gay little thick one that lay down)
Against sky so bright its light reared out—
White needles shifted in splintering crystal.

A small beast ran by—long, pale tongue close to the ground—
Eyes surprised, regurgitating light in lids
Like fish-flesh, dead—disappeared. A dog-
Opera coming near till somewhere someone screamed:
"Treed!"—Men darted, bobbed through far trees
Spreading red stuff in the sun. Silence. Then sound
Like a great, sobbing axe-cry struck everywhere.
My friend threw down his sneering pink plaster
Mask of Wall Street, my girl and I
Our high protest-thing THE BLOOD AND DEATH MACHINE.
We ran a last, bare reach to the quarry.

Trees and grass dancing perilously above stone—
Cut on cut, blanked by scarrifying light.
Our whispers mingled with the strange applause
Of leaves, chaste stammer of grass lashing grass:

"Oh! Oh! I feel like a rabbit. His eyes. The *eyes!*
No eyes like that before. My groin feels cold." The field
Grinned at us with rocks—one a shaped, shining "M"
Mothy was near—straight, shadowy. His words:
"You are the first generation of youth
Not to be trapped in the nervous system.
An ancient and majestic wilderness awaits.
My drug will take your wounded spirit where
It opens into endless God!" His voice seemed
Heard over water, or long ago. *"Remember,*
Between what one thinks and how one acts or
Fails to falls the middle-class, middle-aged
Monolith that tries to take away the right
To live human, prehuman and even
Subhuman adventure to the limit
Of nature. These cubes of orange, red and green
Are all that stands between their cruelty, our will—"
He rolled them on a rock like dice. We took.

*   *   *

Mothy, with an air of knowing mist
Not quite rain blowing: *"Let go, like this lovely drift*
Hiding white, enormous shapes, hard
And enduring as your pride—fear nothing."
The small circle of her final,
Fierce face turned—pale, pure—toward my friend.
His slate-blind eyes and slack poor-mouthed face
Seemed to protest everything, then tensed
In a smile showed complete understanding
(Without a lineament or trace of what)
Until blank features twisted sullen again—

As if by a little, mobile vacuum.
My teeth were trying to eat my tongue. *Clouds,*

Continents of fear turning into calm islands,
Whose grace was wrong except at first sight.
Walking up icy rock gripped by my hands.
Others climbed below—dirty, little ghosts.
I pulled over the top. Black night soared above
A blue too blue—insufferably throbbing—
Somehow around (not through) dark distances.
Then yellow lines of lightning meandering,
Outlined and lit mountains! It all gave way

To mist that stood, rushed off—revealing rock
Was *quiet strength amid forgetfulness* and
Light *nothing but the world's nakedness.*
I saw *trees, all in some way ugly.*
And so were the people there. Mothy:
As it beaked light, his bird-face broke in half.
My girl's back halved by a line of shadow
That grew as if wings were spreading below.
Wings for killing or love? Her body's small,
But willing gesture at my friend answered.
He made membranous then clacking words:
"Now I am on sparkling cement which has red
Letters like deep-cut wounds I cannot read.
A Beelzebub with a blubber-lip!
Ears red wood, dead. Charcoal-chunk hands, clenched.
Eye-brows straight and thin as eye-patch string.
Those big, yellow golf-ball eyes! Restlessly spiteful,

Humiliated he must see me . . ." Mothy said:
"He is your ego-death. Die slow!" (That "death"
Is really guilty pain at ego becoming
Everything, all.) Sun swung through wrecked mist.

A flat bi-valve rock form opened
Darker than shadow ahead. A low darkness sped
And clattered—all dream, but the truth
Of it beautiful, there—*the Minotaur!*
Cubed, orange-fire eyes whose charnel look was fed
Deep with surprise. I realized I
Charmed him because I smelled and dazzled of life—
My plumes mingling colors, of fallen kingdoms!
He had forgotten he thrived by devouring
The lost, alive. Each new death showed him
Death before it died: a pale, shallow face
Distorted on an empty surface. The eyes
Stared at miracle, then staggered, black—
As I twisted in my cormorant-spined steel.
His last words bubbled through blood darkening
(A hoard of human heads and limbs, rooted-
Up crops and levelled orchard-walls)
On acrid floor: *"I had to speak to someone."*

Like blood, I wanted blood to touch me and be wise.
Slippings of paradise pouring from his head . . .
                    *   *   *
Then while that portico of hell still shone
I saw him wandering, horns balancing
A fleshless column of bodies, stacked according
To governments, organizations, institutions

A to Z in a great tottering "I"—
Like a want-ad for a monster lacking
Or losing the designation of God.
"I had to speak to someone" he mooed at sky
Full of red. My little, self-righteous victim!

The sun came out—a golden ingot
With one red spot. My girl lay on stone.
She bent herself to me and cried that she
Was *"unplucked, dream-filled flesh of a rose!"*
Like a fiery parcel my friend moved through
Light sliding colliding inside light.
He seemed to grab all parts of her at once.
She smiled . . . the impact and ardor of
A shooting-star stirring its own departure.

        *   *   *

I was alone, looking at everything bright
That made images of time without will:
Spherical, sublime blue above
A wet shine on rock like memory,
Leaves spinning and dialing the light.

Alone in an inchoate thing which once had been
A meadow—*Mothy was moving in my mind!*
Candescent, sourceful—then dark and coiled
Like a strange, undinal whip whose slow, questioning
Response clothed only by my identity
Was a kind of mouthless kiss! I returned

To the urgent, coastal patterning of sight.
Mothy's face, relaxed into itself
At last—that disappointed, yet sly look

Reckoning on power called middle-age.
"You're *past* it," I said, then sung: *"Down in a meadow*
In an itty bitty poo' swam three
Little fishies and a momma fishie too.
'Swim' she said 'swim if you can'—and they swam
And they swam all over that dam. Boom-boom
Chitum watum—boo!" His snarling, disgusted laugh
In me a minute after he had gone.

The moon was rising. The sun was falling.

———————

I did not join his herd of individuals.
They think he is leading them. The other way.

———————

I want her waiting in a meadow. Wind.
Long dark hair whipping lovely, lazing breasts—
Everything else innocent of all
Except its own shape that proves to be hand-
Shaped as I bring more blood to each place I touch
Until fine, startled bones clutch me and from
A sensual distance of stars a long-
Forgotten God comes, ablaze with pleasure—
Face bright and faceless as the sun—
Riding out dying light, seen everywhere
Majestic, gesturing like cloud on wind.

———————

Talons do not tear any more than masks.

Oh absence, between uncut sky and its floor—
Understand what it is to understand
The world is a place of clouds and slaughter,
Where clear colors of vulgarity run
Beautifully small as they break in the sun
Into a real image of man again:
That quarried emptiness which no sky takes.

Moog's Bar on Snugglepuppy Road

I saw the charge of life and the scar
Of hate on each face—light and dirt—
Alone with my poems at a bar
As if there with a friend alert
To nothing but words. I turned my face
And listened to the sullen accents
Of my tribe. "Unite inner, outer space"
A man mumbled going into the GENTS.
My book in the hand and *mouth* of a girl
Whose skin was like cigar-paper! A thirty-
Year-old dullard at her side with curl-
Ing cupid-shanked lips dancing dirty
Scribbles urged: "You believe it lengthens the time
That drags you along to oblivion
To make your sincerity our curse.
Sincerity cannot be measured in verse,
And guilt can be hid behind meter, rhyme—
But our stare is a stark companion."
She nibbled at a page that was like lettuce-
Leaf. *"I like best the ones stained with letters."*
She pinched my nipple hard. *"You never will
Give to give what the Muse wants—
Obliterating: sycophants,
Youth by itself (a bad companion)
Death—and become a better man."*
She wiped fast at a downy mustache,
And he broke into sweat like a rash.
Triumphant eating shame cannot express!
Drinks dribbled down lips that kissed pieces

Of words, rubble in an abyss.
Faces jammed, quickening speech like birds.
A ritual pattern of breath
In the voices. A sound of death.
I wanted nothing but my lost words.
Pained as if life just born in me whole
Had gone leaving a dead thing with a soul.
I found the door, broke a rough black disc
And walked out into massive green dusk.
The moon was a grave of music and stone.
My body was full of heat and life when
I woke to a sound like a great sobbing
Axe-cry. The room was still. *All the books*
Fallen from their place above my desk
On the floor strangely sheltered in their wrecked shelf.
Gathering them, I saw the words "was robbing"
Typed on a familiar page. *It was this book,*
Awake and alive and quoting itself.

About the Author

Raphael Rudnik was born in New York in 1933. After graduating from Bard College, he worked at a variety of jobs, including several years as a publicity writer for a philanthropic organization. Recently he took his master's degree at Columbia University, and is now a college English instructor.